PORTSMC
CATHEDRAL

THE CATHEDRAL CHURCH OF ST THOMAS OF CANTERBURY

G000269092

Left:
The nave seen from the tower gallery on the occasion of the consecration of the newly-completed cathedral, St Andrew's Day 1991.

Contents

Visitors' Guide	opposite
History Chart	3
A Brief History	4
The Nave	6
The Baptistry and Tower Transepts	10
The Quire and Medieval Transepts	12
The Chapel of St Thomas	16
The Navy Aisle	19
Provost's Postscript	21

Right:
The original 'Golden Barque' weather vane, dated 1710. This was paid for by fees from 'Special Celebrations of the Sacrament' required by the Test Act. The barque now on the cupola of the tower is a copy made in 1953.

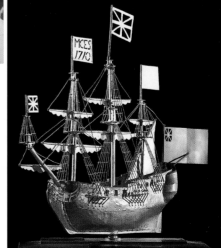

*c.*1180	Jean de Gisors grants land to build a chapel.	1662	Charles II marries Catherine of Braganza in nearby Domus Dei church.
1188	Richard Toclyve consecrates chancel and nave.	1693	New nave and west tower completed.
1196	Godfrey de Lucy consecrates transepts, altars and churchyard.	1902–4	The church is closed for restoration.
1337	The church survives a French raid.	1927	The Diocese of Portsmouth is created.
1449	The Bishop of Chichester is murdered by local sailors. The town's inhabitants are excommunicated and the church closed.	1932	Sir Charles Nicholson publishes plans to enlarge St Thomas's.
		1939	Work stops on the extension scheme.
1591	Elizabeth I worships in St Thomas's.	1990	Work begins on the completion scheme.
1642	The church is bombarded by Parliamentarian forces during the Civil War.	1991	The completed building is consecrated in the presence of HM Queen Elizabeth the Queen Mother.

A Brief History

Around the year 1180 Jean de Gisors, a wealthy Norman merchant, provided land so that the monks of Southwick Priory could build a chapel 'to the glorious honour of the martyr Thomas of Canterbury, one time Archbishop, on my land which is called Sudewede, the island of Portsea'. From humble beginnings, this chapel was to become in turn a parish church in the 14th century and a cathedral church in the 20th century.

The medieval building, which served the sea-faring community based on the Camber, was cruciform with a central tower. Of this building, the transepts and chancel remain.

The medieval building suffered badly in the Civil War. Jean de Gisors' church had a low central tower, spanning the space between two medieval transepts. It was used as a lookout post and lighthouse in times of both peace and war. When the Parliamentary forces attacked the town in 1642, the Royalist garrison used the tower to observe the movements of the enemy forces. Consequently the Parliamentary gunners, positioned across the harbour in Gosport and using artillery from the royal yacht, aimed at the tower and inflicted damage on the church. This,

Above:
An aerial view of the cathedral. To the left lies the Camber, the medieval harbour. At the top can be seen HMS Warrior berthed at the entrance to the dockyard.

Right:
An early photograph of the then parish church showing the heavy concentration of pews, even in the chancel, and the pulpit shorn of its canopy.

Right:
The western towers of the cathedral were built to the designs of Michael Drury by Waring Contractors Ltd. The craftsmanship and materials used echo the work carried out in the 1930s. There is, for instance, no cladding, but a true stone facing to the building.

combined with a subsequent period of neglect, led to the ruin of the medieval tower and nave.

With the restoration of the monarchy came a new period of prosperity and expansion for the borough and dock-yard. In 1683 Charles II authorized a Brief, licensing a collection in churches throughout the land, to raise the £9,000 that was required to rebuild the tower and nave. By 1691 the tower was finished,

the nave being completed in 1693. To cater for increasing congregations, galleries in the transepts were added in 1708 and extended in 1750.

The wooden cupola, with a lantern for shipping on top, was added to the tower in 1703. A ring of eight bells was presented at the same time. Two additional bells were cast in 1957.

The church was closed in 1902 for two years in order that much-needed

Left:
Until after the Second World War, the cathedral was almost invisible from the High Street. Shops and houses hemmed it in on three sides. These were eventually purchased and demolished to give the view we have today.

work on the foundations could take place. During this period St Mary's Colewort, a Chapel of Ease, was fully licensed as the temporary parish church. St Mary's closed in 1906 and after various uses as a warehouse and store it was finally demolished.

In 1927, a new Diocese of Portsmouth was created, carved out of the Diocese of Winchester. On 1 May of that year the parish church of St Thomas of Canterbury became its pro-cathedral. By 1935 the 'provisional' nature of its title had been dropped. At a chapter meeting in October 1932 a first sketch plan for an extension to the church was submitted by Sir Charles Nicholson.

The Nave

When the parish church of St Thomas was chosen to be the cathedral for the new Diocese of Portsmouth, Sir Charles Nicholson, the eminent architect, was called upon to extend the church to a size that would dignify its new status.

Nicholson worked on other parish church cathedrals in England, including Sheffield which, like Portsmouth, was never finished to his design. It is clear from his correspondence with the cathedral authorities that he wished to begin work by constructing a new nave. The authorities, no doubt driven by medieval precedent, disagreed and instead work began at the east end of the building, moving west.

The style that Nicholson chose is that of a round-arched Rhenish Romanesque which echoes the quire of the church with its late 17th-century classical design.

Right: ⑤
The *Christus*. This sculpture is the work of Peter Eugene Ball. It is carved from a piece of oak driftwood and is covered in places with gold leaf.

Opposite: ③
The nave seen from the north transept. It incorporates elements of Nicholson's original unbuilt scheme. The twin turrets flank a singing gallery which faces the nave above the west door. Above this again is a rose window inspired by Nicholson's early drawings.

Right: ③
It is probable that the medieval font, which stands today near the north door in the nave, was provided in 1508, for in this year the church was reopened after many years of closure. Sixty years previously the people of Portsmouth had murdered Adam Moleyns, the Bishop of Chichester, and as a result were excommunicated. The parish church was closed and the people denied the sacraments. The existing font was probably smashed at the time of this outrage and so in 1508 a replacement was needed.

By 1939 the outer quire aisles, the tower transepts and three bays of the nave had been completed. The base of the 17th-century tower had been pierced to form the tower arch. The outbreak of the Second World War then prohibited any further work and the completed bays of the nave were closed off with a brick wall that was intended to be only temporary. As things transpired it was to stay there for over 50 years. Attempts to finish the structure in the 1960s proved unsuccessful.

In 1983 a decision was taken by the cathedral authorities to complete the building and Michael Drury was appointed architect to the project. His first task was to find a solution to the problem of finishing Sir Charles Nicholson's truncated nave. It is therefore through Drury's work at the western end that the visitor now enters the cathedral.

The completed nave is a square space that is encircled by an outer ambulatory or walkway. The ambulatory is low and vaulted and gives us little hint of the wide, sunlit area soon to be encountered in the nave proper.

Right:
The exterior of the cathedral seen from the south-east, showing the medieval transept and chancel to the right. Sir Charles Nicholson's transept flanks the 1691 tower with Michael Drury's west towers to the left.

Left: ⑤
The tower arch seen from the nave. The organ case, originally built to house an instrument by Abraham Jordan, dates from 1718. It now faces east into the quire, in front of an organ by John Nicholson, built 1855–61 for Manchester Cathedral.

Below right:
The Bishop of Portsmouth presides over a service of Ordination in the nave.

With no fixed furniture, the nave has the feeling of a gathering space, a market place. In this sense it is rather like the atrium in front of an early Roman basilica. Here people gathered before worship – it was an enlarged entrance hall.

There is a strong feeling in the nave that we are 'outside' the main body of the church, which we glimpse when we look east through the tunnel under the tower and through the transepts. We could be left behind here if we don't make the decision to push on east. It is here, for instance, that the congregation gathers for the Easter vigil. In the darkness of the nave they wait, telling stories of their past and of God's redeeming power. Before redemption must come death and resurrection. So the triumphant *Christus*, Peter Ball's sculpture in gilded wood, beckons the pilgrim to share the death and resurrection of baptism.

The Baptistry and Tower Transepts

The dominant feature of the south tower transept is the bronze statue of St John the Baptist, by David Wynne. It was cast in 1951 as a memorial to a Winchester College boy killed on the Matterhorn.

Here also is the painting *The Miraculous Draught of Fishes* by W.L. Wyllie, the celebrated marine artist, who lived locally.

The north tower transept houses one of Sir Charles Nicholson's gifts to the cathedral, the ceramic plaque of the Virgin and Child by Andrea della Robbia (1435–1525), the Florentine sculptor.

The tower is pierced to provide an organ gallery raised on a low, dark passage. The new font, made to a Greek design of the 9th century, is placed centrally under the tower, that link between the newly completed nave and the quire of the 17th-century church. It is there for a purpose. That narrow space under the tower is the hinge between the two main parts of the building: the narrow, dark gateway between the outer world of the nave and the celebrating church, gathered round lectern and altar, word and

Right: ④
A memorial to Sir Charles Blount (1568–1600) recording a promising career cut short by a premature death. It is the oldest monument in the cathedral.

Below: ⑥
The font, as seen from the quire. The cathedral staff are assisted each day by volunteer clergy from the diocese in their work of welcome and care for the many people who visit the cathedral. Someone is always on hand to offer counsel or advice when requested, and one such volunteer is seen here on duty.

sacrament, in the quire. Traditionally, fonts have been associated with the principal entrance of the church, as a reminder of our entry into Christ.

It has been said that the font looks like a coffin! In one sense it is. Baptism is the way in which Christian people of all ages share Christ's death in order that they may be raised to his new life. Passing through the waters of baptism marks our freedom from the slavery of self and sin and our entry into God's promised land where we are nourished by word and sacrament. But that dramatic passing from death to life is also understood to be a moment of new birth, the point when our Christian discipleship takes a decisive step on the path to maturity. The inscription around the rim of the stone font reminds us of this – as we mount the steps that lead to the font, we remember that all the promises made at our baptism required some movement in us:

I turn to Christ.
I repent of my sins.
I renounce evil.

Thy nativity, O Mother of God,
Has brought joy to all the world:
For from thee has shone forth
The Sun of Righteousness,
Christ our God.
He has loosed us from the curse, and
given the blessing: He has vanquished death,
and bestowed on us eternal life.

THE ORTHODOX LITURGY

Top: ④
A ceramic plaque of
the Virgin and Child by
Andrea della Robbia.

Above:
A service of baptism.

'When you went down into the water, it was like night and you
could see nothing: but when you came up again
it was like finding yourself in the day.
That one moment was your death and your birth:
that saving water was both your grave and your mother.'

FONT INSCRIPTION FROM CYRIL OF JERUSALEM

The Quire and Medieval Transepts

Above:
A contemporary print of the interior as it was in the early 19th century. Note the galleries in the transepts, the flat ceiling in the chancel and the Duke of Buckingham's memorial in its former position on the east wall of the church.

Right and Far right: ⑨
The two lower lights of the 'D-Day' window in the Holy Martyrs Chapel. They depict the two most famous seaborne actions of the Second World War; the rescue of British troops at the evacuation of Dunkirk in May–June 1940 and the landing of Allied forces in Normandy on D-Day, June 1944. They are a memorial to Admiral Sir Bertram Ramsay who commanded the seaborne forces in both actions, and are the work of Messrs. Edwards & Powell.

The quire of the cathedral is, in essence, the nave of the former parish church. Rebuilt in the 1690s it has the feel of a classical Wren church.

In the recent reordering of furniture, care has been taken to clarify the homely clutter of cut-down box pews and to recreate the more elegant atmosphere of an 18th-century church. The pews are arranged as in an Oxford or Cambridge college, and the installation of modern candelabra echoes the classical feel of the building. The organ case belongs to the instrument which was installed by Abraham Jordan in 1718. The new podium for the principal altar is of Purbeck stone. The mosaic work throughout the cathedral is by Richard Noviss.

The medieval transepts were open to the rafters until 1992 when flat classical ceilings were inserted to harmonize with the quire. The south quire transept is formed out of one of the arms of the first cross-shaped church. Consecrated in 1196, its altar was dedicated to St John the Baptist and several other martyrs. It is consequently known as the Holy Martyrs Chapel. The statue of St Sebastian above the altar is the work of a local sculptor, John Phillipson.

heavy wooden shutters which acted as a covering before the days of glass.

The windows in the chapel are of considerable local interest. The upper lancet window in the Holy Martyrs Chapel was the gift of the D-Day and Normandy Fellowship in 1984, the 40th anniversary of the D-Day and Normandy landings. A bronze plaque on the panelling recalls the visit of Her Majesty Queen Elizabeth the Queen Mother to the cathedral on the occasion of the dedication of the window by the then Archbishop of Canterbury,

This part of the building was originally vaulted in stone and the lines of the vaulting can still be traced on the walls. In the south-west corner of the chapel is a door that leads to the stairs which serve the clerestory passage. This passage was probably used to give access to the window spaces for the opening and closing of the

Left:
The royal arms of William and Mary are fixed to the pillar above the Corporation Pew in the quire. This box pew, the last in the cathedral with a door, is the official seat of the Lord Mayor of Portsmouth. The cathedral is the civic church of the city.

Dr Robert Runcie. The three panel altar piece, or triptych, is the work of the sculptor Edward Robinson. Its forbidding exterior opens to reveal shafts of resurrection light.

The north quire transept has on its east wall a 13th-century painting of the Last Judgment, showing Christ in Majesty assisted by the heavenly hosts.

In the quire of the cathedral we reach the worshipping core of the building. The balance between word and sacrament is found here in the lectern and the principal altar. These are the twin foci of any celebration of the Eucharist, the sacrament which is at the centre of our common life and worship. In this space the regular congregation meets for worship.

And Shew my
people their
Transgressions
And the house
of JACOB their
SINS

The cathedral serves both a parish of 5,000 souls and a diocese of many thousands more. Its role is to cater for the needs of both, providing the focus for the Bishop of Portsmouth's pastoral and teaching ministry in his diocese and the worshipping centre expected by the local population.

The word 'cathedral' comes from the Greek word for a seat, *kathedra*. It is in his cathedral that the bishop of a diocese keeps his seat or throne. The Bishop of Portsmouth's chair stands against the crossing pillar to the north of the principal altar. The significance of this seat in the cathedral emphasizes the Bishop's ministry as a focus of unity in the diocese. It is also his 'teaching' seat from which, as pastor of his flock, he guides and disciplines those in his care.

Above: ⑩
The goddess of Fame (1693) from above the pulpit. Her banner quotes Isaiah 58: 'Cry aloud, Spare not, Lift up thy voice like a trumpet and shew my people their transgressions, And the house of Jacob their sins.'

Above right: ⑪
The Bishop's chair is of the William and Mary period and is a memorial to Michael Nott (Provost 1972–82). Above it hang the arms of the diocese. These include the cross-keys and sword of the mother diocese of Winchester.

Left:
The quire and the chancel.

Right:
The Bishop, seated on the throne, presides at a celebration of the Eucharist.

The Chapel of St Thomas

Right: ⑩
The monument (1631)
to George Villiers, Duke
of Buckingham.

Far right: ⑬
The chancel, with the
tester (canopy) and pyx.

Below: ⑬
The lancet window at
the east end.

The original chancel is of exceptional architectural interest. Built no later than 1185, it demonstrates the transitional period when the Norman or Romanesque style of architecture was giving place to the more French Gothic, known in this country as Early English. Each main arched space of the chancel encloses a pair of pointed Gothic arches. The use of Purbeck marble in the pillars of the clerestory looks forward to its more sophisticated use in Salisbury Cathedral and Westminster Abbey. This part of the cathedral underwent extensive but sensitive reconstruction in 1843, possibly at the hands of the architect Livesay.

Livesay removed the Wren-like chancel arch, inserting the present Gothic design. He also removed a rather uninspired flat classical ceiling and constructed the lath and plaster vaulting we see now. For the period it was a highly informed piece of archaeological reconstruction. The chancel therefore in most respects looks the same as when it was first erected. The substitution of black polished Irish marble for the original Purbeck in the lower arcading is unfortunate, but one of the columns had already been replaced with a cast-iron dummy in 1843. With the reconstruction of 1904 the other columns were found to be incapable of bearing the weight demanded of them, and so were removed and replaced.

Apart from Boxgrove Priory in Sussex, possibly the work of the same mason at a slightly later date, no other parish church in the country has an east end with side aisles of this particular design.

In the east wall is a pointed arch, discovered when the mid 19th-century reredos was removed, recessed in an unusual way to half the thickness of the wall. The small lancet window, with its wide inward splay, is Norman and was restored in 1920, having been blocked up for a long period. Below the window is a ledger slab commemorating Benjamin Burgess, the minister appointed to serve the church during the Commonwealth (1649–60). The cost of moving the monument to its present position in 1904 was borne by the Nonconformist ministers of the city.

In the south chancel aisle is the large monument in black and white marble to George Villiers, Duke of Buckingham, a favourite of Charles I. This monument stood in the centre of the east wall of the sanctuary, in the place of a reredos! It was moved in the 1843 reconstruction. Possibly the work of Nicholas Stone, it was erected by Villiers' sister, the Countess of Denbigh, in 1631. The inscription tells of Buckingham's murder at the hands of one John Felton, an embittered sea captain, at 11 High Street, Portsmouth on 23 August, 1628.

Felton, angry because Villiers had not given him command of a ship, mingled with the crowd that surrounded the Duke after he had taken breakfast. It was easy for Felton to stab him, but not so easy to effect an escape. The Duke is buried in Westminster Abbey, but as the inscription tells, in a somewhat macabre fashion, his bowels lie buried in the cathedral.

The two coloured monuments at the east end of this aisle are of great interest to naval historians. They commemorate Colonel William Willoughby and Robert Moulton, Commissioners of the Admiralty during the Commonwealth. From 1649 to 1652 they restored the dockyard and recommended shipbuilding there after an interval of 141 years. The American connection is also seen here in the bronze plaque to Captain John Mason, the founder of the state of New Hampshire. It was in Mason's house that the Duke of Buckingham was murdered.

At the heart of this chapel hangs the tester, or wooden canopy, dating from 1939. From it hangs what appears to be a silver and gilt crown. This is a hanging pyx, designed by Hector Miller, in which consecrated bread and wine of the Eucharist are reserved. Jesus said, 'Do this in remembrance of me' and so the pyx containing the elements of the Sacrament is a focus of Christ's presence amongst us, yet lifted up from us. For it is Christ who has gone on before us to prepare a place for us, 'who ever lives to make intercession for us'.

God does not call us simply to be members of his church, he calls us to move beyond that, to recognize that he is Lord, not only of the church but of the whole world, and that his kingdom extends beyond anything that we can conceive or understand. To this end we are compelled to think beyond the cathedral building itself, out into the world at large.

Below: ⑭
The Peace Globe is based on a design from Stockholm Cathedral. It was made in 1985 by students of Highbury College of Technology. The globe is still while at its heart rotates the cross, symbol of despair and of hope. Quite often it is difficult to put a prayer felt into words. The simple action of lighting a candle focuses the thought and expresses the prayer in a concrete form.

The Navy Aisle

This aisle, one of the first sections of Nicholson's extension plan to be finished, was partly paid for by donations received from officers and men of the Royal Navy. From its foundation, the church has had close connections with the seafaring community and later the Royal Navy. It was here that naval commanders received communion before taking their first appointment, as required by law until 1828 when the Test Act was repealed.

The monument to Admiral Sir John Kempthorne is a link with the name of 'Mary Rose'. His ship *Mary Rose*, a model of which hangs in the aisle, defeated seven Algerine pirate vessels in 1669. It is therefore fitting that this aisle was chosen as the site for the grave of a crew member of Henry VIII's flag ship *Mary Rose* which foundered in the Solent on 19 July 1545.

On Thursday 19 July 1984, almost 450 years after the ship went down, a Requiem Mass was celebrated in the cathedral for the crew. The stone marking the grave is of Welsh slate and is the work of John Skelton.

Also in this aisle is the memorial by John Shaw to the crew of the Portsmouth fishing vessel *Wilhelmina J* which was lost at sea in 1991.

Right: ⑧
Beneath this stone set in the floor of the Navy Aisle lie the bones of a crew member of Henry VIII's flagship *Mary Rose*. These were discovered when the ship was brought to the surface of the Solent in 1982, prior to restoration in Portsmouth.

Below left: ⑧
The memorial to to the crew of the fishing vessel *Wilhelmina J.*

Below: ⑦
The cathedral bookshop with the Navy Aisle beyond.

Above:
The Holy Communion is administered at the altar in the quire.

Right:
A children's workshop, part of the cathedral's extended ministry.